Horse
Stories
that
Really Happened

Horse
Stories
that
Really Happened

Diana Kimpton

Illustrated by Eric Robson

Hippo

I would like to thank the many people who have helped me find the stories in this book, especially Grace Bussell's family, the Western Australian Historical Society, John Buckingham, the RSPCA, Chief Inspector John Paul and Angela Morran. D.K.

Scholastic Children's Books,
Commonwealth House, 1-19 New Oxford Street,
London WC1A 1NU, UK

A division of Scholastic Ltd
London ~ New York ~ Toronto ~ Sydney ~ Auckland
Mexico City ~ New Delhi ~ Hong Kong

Published in the UK by Scholastic Ltd, 1999

Text copyright © Diana Kimpton, 1999
Illustrations copyright © Eric Robson, 1999

ISBN 0 590 11102 7

All rights reserved
Typeset by Falcon Oast Graphic Art Ltd.
Printed and bound by Bath Press, Bath.

2 4 6 8 10 9 7 5 3

The right of Diana Kimpton and Eric Robson to be identified as the author
and illustrator of this work respectively has been asserted by them in
accordance with the Copyright, Designs and Patents Act, 1988.

Contents

Before you begin...

The stories in this book come from many different places and different times. But they are all about my favourite animals – horses.

Within these pages, you will meet racehorses and wild horses. You will read stories of great courage and tales of the wonderful friendship which can exist between humans and horses. In addition, at the end of each story, you will find a *Did You Know...?* section full of facts about these wonderful animals.

All these stories really happened. Of course, I wasn't there at the time so I don't know every single detail of who did what and what was said. To make the stories complete and fun to read, I have used my imagination to fill in the gaps. I've invented the conversations, other details and some of the characters.

I hope you enjoy reading them as much as I enjoyed writing them.

Diana Kimpton

The Taming of Bucephalus

Macedonia, near Greece, 345 bc

Alexander stood in the shadows away from the hot sun and watched the horse. It was no beauty. Its huge eyes and wide forehead gave it a face like an ox.

But those same eyes were full of spirit and a love of life. Strong muscles rippled under its gleaming black coat. It was the most wonderful horse Alexander had ever seen.

He watched as his father and the other

men inspected the animal. He wished he could be with them but he knew they would say he was too young.

The horse watched the men too. It flared its nostrils and stamped its feet nervously. It didn't know or care that Alexander's father was a king – the most powerful king that Macedonia had ever had.

The man holding the horse smiled.

"He's exactly what you need, Your Majesty. He's strong and fit and he runs as fast as the wind."

"But he looks as wild and restless as the wind too," said the king. "He hasn't stopped fidgeting and pawing the ground since he arrived. He will be no use to me if he can't be ridden."

Alexander was alarmed at the thought of his father sending this wonderful horse away. Then he relaxed as he saw Demetrius step forward. Demetrius was in charge of the cavalry and one of the best riders in the whole country. He was sure to be able to ride the black stallion.

The animal shifted nervously from foot to foot as Demetrius walked towards it and took hold of the reins. It calmed a little when he patted its neck but that calm disappeared as soon as Demetrius sprang on to its bare back.

The horse raised its head in alarm, rolled its eyes and stepped backwards as if it was trying to escape from something terrifying in front of it. Then it reared up high on its back legs, pawing at the air with its front hooves.

For a moment, it looked as if it would fall over backwards. But it didn't. It crashed down to the ground and immediately put its head between its knees. It arched its back and kicked out with its back legs in an enormous buck.

That first buck was followed by another and another. Demetrius clung on tightly and tried to pull the horse's head up with the reins. The animal swung sharply to the right and then the left, throwing its rider off balance.

Before he could steady himself, the horse reared again. This time Demetrius couldn't stay on. He slipped backwards off the horse and rolled on the ground to get clear of its hooves.

Some of the watching crowd laughed.

Demetrius clambered to his feet and scowled at them. "So which of you is going to do better?" he asked.

The king looked thoughtfully at the waiting men. "Let Parmenion try," he said. "He's the best race rider I have ever seen."

A tall, thin man stepped out of the

crowd and walked slowly towards the horse. The black stallion watched him warily as he approached. It danced nervously from foot to foot and Alexander noticed that its shadow danced with it.

As soon as Parmenion was close enough, he grabbed the reins and leapt nimbly on to the horse's back. The horse stepped backwards in alarm just as it had done before but this time Alexander could see what it was frightened of.

On the dusty ground in front of the horse lay its own shadow – a shadow changed by the rider on its back into a terrifying two-headed monster.

The horse continued to back away and the shadow moved with it. Parmenion urged the animal forward but it was too frightened to obey. Instead it started to twist and buck to get rid of its rider.

Parmenion hung on to the black mane and gripped hard with his bare legs in an attempt to stay on. He succeeded longer than Demetrius had done, but eventually he too lost his balance. Finally one enormous buck sent him flying through the air to land in a heap at the king's feet while the horse keeper caught hold of the reins before the stallion could escape.

 There was no laughter this time. It was a bad fall and, for a moment, Alexander was frightened that the rider was badly hurt. But then Parmenion climbed slowly to his feet. He was rubbing his shoulder but otherwise seemed uninjured.

"I've seen enough," said the king. "The horse is unrideable. It will have to go."

"No! No!" cried Alexander. "Look at how strong it is. See how its coat gleams in the sun. It's the most wonderful horse I've ever seen. You can't get rid of it."

"Yes, I can. There's no point in keeping a useless horse."

Alexander bit his lip thoughtfully as he wondered how to change his father's mind. Then he looked again at the restless horse with its dancing shadow and he had an idea.

"Let me try to ride it," he said. "I'm sure I can do it."

Alexander's father laughed and so did everyone else.

"You!" said Demetrius. "But you're only a child."

Alexander stood up as tall as he could. "I'm eleven," he said. "And I'm sure I can ride that horse."

Alexander's father laughed again. "You're right about your age anyway," he said. "And I admire your courage. Go ahead and try. You can't do any worse than the other two."

Alexander walked slowly towards the black stallion and took the reins. But he didn't leap straight on to its back as Parmenion had done. Instead he turned the horse round until it was facing the sun. Its shadow was still there but it was behind it now so the horse couldn't see it.

Alexander talked softly to the animal, stroking its mane and neck as he spoke. The horse gradually relaxed and, for the first time, stopped its restless movements and stood still.

Very gently Alexander ran his hands over the horse's back. It quivered slightly at his touch but stayed calm. He pressed harder. The horse still didn't move.

Finally he took hold of the mane with one hand and leapt on to its back. The horse took one step backwards, staring at the ground, looking for the monster that had frightened it before. But this time there was no monster – just the bare, sunlit earth.

Alexander sat very still. He could feel the tension in the horse's body. He knew one wrong move could set off the rearing and bucking which had made the others fall.

He talked softly to the horse and it flicked back its ears to listen. Then he reached forward very slowly and stroked its neck. Gradually he felt the tension go out of its muscles as the horse relaxed and started to trust him.

When he was sure the horse was calm, he pressed his legs against its sides and urged it forward. At the same time, he used the reins to make sure it moved towards the sun. He still didn't want it to see its shadow.

The horse walked forward slowly and hesitantly at first but it soon grew more confident and stepped out willingly. Alexander urged it into a trot and then a canter. Soon they were galloping together through the fields and the olive groves.

Alexander had never ridden such a wonderful horse before. It felt as if they could gallop on for ever. But he knew they couldn't. Reluctantly he pulled the horse to a halt. It was time to turn back towards home and he knew this would be the real test of the horse because then the sun would be behind them.

The black stallion turned willingly in response to his hands on the reins. Then it saw its shadow dancing on the ground in front of it and it hesitated.

Alexander urged it on and, for a moment, he thought the horse was going to rear. But it didn't. Its trust in him overcame its fear and it moved forwards willingly.

The gallop home was even better than the first one. This time Alexander knew he had succeeded. He could just relax and enjoy the pleasure of the ride until he pulled the horse to a halt in front of his father.

The king's eyes shone with pride. "That was a wonderful achievement, my son," he said. "I think one day you will be an even greater king than I am."

"So you'll keep the horse," said Alexander.

"No," said his father. "I'll give him to you. A great king will need a great horse and you'd better choose a great name for him."

Alexander was delighted. "I'll keep him for ever," he said. "And I'll call him Bucephalus."

His father looked puzzled. "But that means ox-head," he said.

"I know," explained Alexander as he stroked the horse's neck. "He's got a face like an ox and now he has a name to go with it."

Bucephalus carried Alexander for many years and never let anyone else ride him. When Alexander grew up, he became a great ruler just like his father predicted and conquered a huge empire. He became known throughout the world as Alexander the Great and Bucephalus became the first famous horse in history.

Did you know…?

Saddles and stirrups

1. Alexander rode bareback like most other people at that time. Even if he had had a saddle, he wouldn't have had any stirrups as they weren't invented until hundreds of years later. No one is quite sure who first thought of them but everyone agrees that their invention transformed riding as it made falling off a much less frequent event.

2. You need different length stirrups for different styles of riding – long ones for western riding to help you sit deep in the saddle and short ones for jumping to help you lean forward over the jumps. To find

the right length for ordinary riding, take your feet out of the stirrups and let your legs hang down loosely. The bottom of the stirrups should be level with your ankle-bones.

3. Inside every saddle is a solid frame called a saddle-tree which gives the saddle its shape and keeps the rider's weight off the horse's spine. The tree always used to be made of wood, but now it is sometimes made of plastic or fibreglass instead.

4. Horses like to roll to scratch their backs, especially when they have just been ridden. But never let your horse roll with its saddle on it. It may break the saddle-tree and then the saddle will be useless because

it will hurt the horse's back. If you are holding a saddled horse that starts to sag at the knees so it can roll, you can stop it by making it walk forwards instead.

5. In the past, women used to ride side-saddle. This is not as hard as it looks because a side-saddle is very different from an ordinary saddle. Hidden under the rider's skirts are two horns – the rider's right leg goes over the top one and her left leg under the bottom one. If she thinks she might fall off, she can stop herself by pushing her legs against the horns.

6. Most horses are ridden with a bit in their mouths to allow the rider to control the horse. But some horses are happier ridden

in a special bridle called a hackamore which has no bit. You use the reins in the normal way but they pull on the horse's nose instead of its mouth.

Saving Savanna

Surrey, England, December 1988

Alison stared at the empty field in dismay. Where was Savanna? Earlier in the morning she had been grazing happily. Now there was no sign of her at all.

She struggled to stay calm as she ran through the drizzly rain, searching for the horse she loved. But deep inside, she felt a rising tide of panic. What could have happened to Savanna? Was she lying somewhere hurt or had thieves come and stolen her?

One by one, Alison checked all the neighbouring fields, hoping to see the dark bay mare. But each time she was disappointed. There was no sign of Savanna anywhere.

Then she heard a sound from the direction of the river. She stopped and listened. The sound came again – a strange groaning noise that sent a shiver of fear down Alison's back. It was the sound of a horse in distress.

She pushed her way through the bushes to the bank and looked down at the fast-flowing river. At first she thought Savanna wasn't there. Then, to her horror, she spotted the tip of her horse's nose sticking up from the water.

Savanna was completely trapped. She must have fallen into the river and sunk in the soft mud at the bottom. She was holding her head up to stop herself drowning but only her nostrils were still above the surface. Her eyes, her ears and all the rest of her body were under water.

RSPCA Inspector John Paul was at home enjoying a day off work when the 'phone rang.

"There's a horse trapped in a river," said the voice at the other end. "Two fire engines have gone to help but they want someone from the RSPCA as quickly as possible."

John grabbed his jacket and ran to his

van. He knew he couldn't afford to waste any time. It was the middle of the winter and the water in the river would be icy cold. The horse wouldn't be able to survive for very long.

One of the firemen was waiting by Savanna's field to show him the way. "My name's Ian," he said as they ran together towards the river. "I'm really glad you've come."

There was a quite a crowd on the bank when they arrived. Ian quickly introduced John to the other firemen and to Alison, who was soaking wet now and shivering despite the shiny, silver space blanket wrapped around her shoulders.

"It's her horse," he explained. "She jumped in the water and managed to put a head collar and rope on it. If she hadn't done that, we wouldn't be able to do anything to help."

"The water's freezing," said Alison. "I was only in there a few minutes but I got so cold I needed help to get out." She looked worried as she added, "Savanna's already been in there much longer than me. She must be even colder."

John nodded and then turned his attention to the horse. The bank was so high that he was looking almost straight down on her. She still had her nose out of the water but she had stopped groaning now. Only the movement of her nostrils showed that she was still alive.

"It's no good," said Ian. "The bank's so high that we can only pull the rope straight upwards. There's no way we're going to get her out like that."

"The mud comes right up past her belly," said Alison in an anxious voice. "I could feel it when I was in there. She's completely helpless. What on earth are we going to do?"

Ian looked thoughtfully at the other side of the river. "If only we could pull her from over there," he said. "We'd be pulling sideways and that might loosen the mud's grip just enough to let her kick her way free."

"And that bank's a bit lower than this one," said John. "It would be easier to get her out on that side. But we'd need a very long rope."

"That's no problem," said Ian. "We've got one of those."

"And we'd have to tie it on her and get it to the other side," continued John.

"That's no problem either," said Ian as he unbuttoned his jacket. He stripped to his underpants, grabbed the rope and jumped into the water. He tied one end to Savanna's head collar and then swam out into the main stream of the river holding the other end in his hand.

John and the others watched anxiously

as he battled his way through the cold, swirling water. It had been raining heavily all night and the river was swollen with flood water. Swimming it was a dangerous activity.

He reached the other side safely and clambered up the bank. Then he took the rope in both hands and pulled as hard as he could. The muscles in his arms bulged with the effort and he dug his heels into the soft ground to stop himself sliding forwards.

At first nothing happened; but Ian didn't stop. He pulled and pulled. Then suddenly the river bed loosened its grip on Savanna. She immediately started to struggle and kick and, in a few seconds, she was free from the clinging mud which had held her prisoner for so long.

Everyone on the river bank cheered with delight. Ian pulled steadily on the rope to encourage her towards him and she half swam and half floated into the middle of the river.

But the horse had no strength left. Without any warning, she stopped swimming and rolled first on to her side and then on to her back. Her legs and belly came out of the water for an instant and then she sank.

John watched with horror as she disappeared from sight and instantly decided what to do. He couldn't leave Savanna to drown. He had to try to save her. So he took off his coat and dived into the icy water.

The river was even colder than he had imagined. It was so cold that it took his breath away. But he couldn't go back now. He had a job to do.

As soon as he came to the surface, he swam to where Ian's rope disappeared into the water. Then he took a huge lungful of air and dived down beside it. He couldn't see anything through the muddy brown water so he followed the rope down, reaching out with his hands to search for Savanna. At first, he found nothing at all. Then suddenly his fingers touched her mane. He felt his way along her neck to her head, grabbed the head collar and fought his way back to the surface.

The horse came up with him but as they neared the surface, she thrashed her legs wildly. John felt a sharp pain as one of her hooves kicked him on the shins and knocked him backwards. To his horror, he felt the head collar tugged out of his fingers. But, luckily, Savanna kept on going upwards and reached the surface only moments before he did.

As soon as his head came above the water, he grabbed hold of the head collar again with one hand and used the other one to swim with. It was hard work. Savanna had completely collapsed and John's swimming had to keep her head above water as well as his own.

While he swam, Ian hauled on Savanna's rope and together they gradually overcame the river's attempt to sweep the horse downstream. As John came close to the bank, the water grew shallower and he felt a gentle bump as Savanna's legs touched the bottom. But he was still out of his depth and becoming more and more tired from the effort of keeping them both afloat.

Then John saw an old tree growing close to the river with branches which hung out over the water. Its roots were thick and strong and some of them stuck out from the bank. He reached out, caught hold of one and held on tightly to stop himself sinking.

Savanna had no energy left to save herself so John put her head over his right shoulder to keep her from drowning. Her body felt completely limp and her eyes were open and staring, but she was still breathing. He had saved her from drowning but his job wasn't finished yet. They still needed to get her out of the water before she died of cold.

He looked back to the opposite bank and saw the others waving. "We're on our way over," they yelled. "We'll be there as soon as we can." They picked up their equipment and pushed their way through the bushes, back towards the waiting fire-engines. John knew they would be as quick as they could; but he also knew that the nearest bridge was several miles away. It would be a long time before they could reach him.

John was determined not to abandon

Savanna. He stayed in the river with her, holding on to the tree root with his hands and supporting her head with his shoulder. As the minutes ticked by, he got colder and colder. His arms and shoulders were exposed to the chill December wind and drizzly rain. The rest of him was under the surface, immersed in water which was only a few degrees above freezing. The icy cold numbed his body and soon he could feel nothing at all from the chest down. It was as if his legs had disappeared.

Eventually he heard the sound of engines and voices and the others arrived. "It's my turn now," said Alison's friend, Toni, as she slipped into the water beside him. "I'll take over while you get out and get warm."

But by now John had been in the water for 40 minutes and he was so cold that he couldn't climb out by himself. The firemen

threw him a rope and Toni helped
him tie it under his arms. Then they
started to pull and John felt himself
slowly come out of the water and up the
bank. His legs and body were so numb that
he didn't even feel the stings as he was
pulled through a clump of stinging nettles.

As soon as he was safely on dry land, the
others wrapped him in space blankets and
helped him into one of the fire-engines to
warm up. It was a huge relief to be out of
the water and, for a while, he concentrated
on getting feeling back into his numb body.

John could clearly see Savanna's head from where he was sitting. But, after ten minutes, she started gradually to disappear from view and John realized to his horror that she was sinking in the mud again.

"Help," shouted Toni. "I can only keep her head up. I can't keep the rest of her up as well."

"We'll have to get a fire hose right round underneath her," said John as he climbed shakily from the fire-engine. "Then we can hold her up to stop her sinking any more and maybe lift her out if we can get something strong enough to pull with."

Some of the firemen went in search of a tractor while John ignored the cold and got back in the river again. But he was too late. Savanna was already more than belly-deep in the mud. He couldn't get his hand or the hose underneath her.

"It's hopeless," said the vet who had  arrived while John was in the water. "There's no way you're going to get her out alive. You're just prolonging her suffering. It would be kinder to shoot her now right where she is."

Everyone looked at him in horror.

"We can't give up now," said Alison.

"Not after everything we've done," said Ian.

"Give us one more try," said John. "Please."

"All right," agreed the vet. "Just one more."

John and the others huddled together and discussed their next move. There was only one thing they hadn't tried yet – pulling Savanna out with a rope tied round her neck.

41

"It's dangerous," explained John. "We might strangle her or break her neck. But if we don't try, she'll die anyway so we've got to take the risk."

As soon as the rope was firmly attached to the horse, they tied the other end to the borrowed tractor and told the driver to start pulling. The rope tightened round her neck. Savanna's eyes bulged and she started to struggle.

"Stop," John yelled to the driver. "She'll break her neck if she struggles like that."

The tractor stopped and Savanna collapsed again. But the pulling had lifted her a little bit out of the mud. "Her front legs are still trapped but they're looser," yelled Toni.

"Can we try once more?" John asked.

The vet nodded in agreement and the tractor moved forward again. This time the horse seemed to know that they were

trying to help. Although her eyes bulged as the rope tightened, she didn't try to struggle against it.

Suddenly one leg came free. She lifted it clear of the mud and got it caught on one of the branches hanging down over the bank. The leg took some of her weight so she was half in and half out of the water. The tractor kept pulling and gradually Savanna's totally limp body came up the bank like a wet rag and slithered on to dry land.

Everyone cheered and immediately

sprang into action. The vet injected her with medicine to keep her heart beating. John and the others massaged her body and covered her with straw and space blankets to warm her up. But the battle wasn't over. She could still die from cold and shock.

Slowly their efforts started to work. Her eyes lost their blank stare, her ears and legs began to move and, after only ten minutes, she heaved herself up to a sitting position.

The sight filled John and the others with hope. They redoubled their efforts and, after more massaging and lots of encouragement, Savanna staggered shakily to her feet. More encouragement got her walking – unsteadily at first but with growing confidence as the movement warmed her body.

Her rescuers watched with satisfaction as they saw the dark bay mare recover before their eyes. They had done the impossible – they had saved Savanna.

For John, Ian and the others, seeing Savanna safe was the best reward they could have had for all their efforts. But it wasn't the only one they got. Six months later, Princess Anne presented John, Ian, Alison and Toni with the RSPCA silver medal for bravery. She also gave bronze medals to the other firemen and a certificate of commendation to the tractor driver.

Savanna met the Princess too and ate her posy of flowers.

Did you know....?

Looking after horses

1. A pony is much more difficult and expensive to look after than a cat or a hamster. It also needs far more space and grass than most people have in their back garden. So don't get a pony of your own unless you are sure you can care for it properly and you can afford to pay all the bills.

2. Horses have small stomachs so they like to eat little and often. Given the chance, they will spend as long as 15 hours a day eating, and in the process they get through large quantities of food. Even a small pony will need more than two bales of hay each

week when the grass stops growing in the winter.

3. Hooves are like huge toenails so it doesn't hurt the horse when the farrier trims them or nails on the shoes. The shoes stop the hooves wearing down too fast on hard ground and need to be replaced every four to six weeks. Even if they are not worn out, the hooves will have grown so much that the old shoes don't fit properly.

4. Hay and straw can be dusty. If you are looking after a horse with a cough, damp the hay before you put it in the stable and use dust-free bedding. Wood shavings are good, but be careful when you muck out. Wet shavings are so heavy that you might

not be able to push the wheelbarrow if you fill it right up.

5. Horses can drink more than 40 litres of water a day so they need to have water available all the time. If you are looking after a pony in a stable, you must make sure its buckets are always full. If it lives in a field, you must go out on cold, winter mornings to break the ice on the trough.

6. If a pony is lame and its hooves feel warm, it may have laminitis or founder, which is often caused by too much rich food. This is extremely painful and can cause long-term problems, so ask a vet what to do and follow their advice carefully.

Dancing for their Lives

St Martin, Austria, May 1945

As Kurt ran through the streets of St Martin to the stables, the village was quieter than it had been for weeks. The war – later to be known as the Second World War – which had raged across Europe was coming to an end. There was no more rumble of distant guns and no throb of aircraft engines overhead. Most of all, the constant tramp of marching feet had stopped. The retreating

German army had poured through the village during the night, but now all the soldiers had gone, taking the fighting with them.

An old man carrying a rusty rifle stepped into his path. "Where are you off to in such a hurry, lad?" he asked.

"To see the white horses," said Kurt. "I help clean the stables."

"Well, make the most of it, lad," he said. "The Americans are coming and who knows what will happen then. Food's short and horse meat tastes good."

The old man's words sent a shiver of fear down Kurt's back. The horses had come to St Martin for safety, away from the bombs falling on Vienna. But everything was in chaos now. Perhaps they weren't safe here any more.

He started to run even faster, his heart racing with fear. As soon as he reached the stables, he rushed inside and was relieved to find that everything was normal. The white stallions were calmly munching their hay as if this was just an ordinary day. They knew nothing of the war or the danger they were in.

One of the men looking after the horses waved at Kurt. "You're late today," he said. "It's nearly time for lunch."

"I'm sorry, Max," said Kurt. "Mum wouldn't let me out at first. She said it wasn't safe."

Max smiled. "Don't worry," he said. "Come and say hello to Africa. He's been waiting for you."

Kurt reached in his pocket and pulled out a handful of grass he had picked from the roadside. He put it on the palm of his hand and held it out to the white stallion Max was grooming.

"That's right," said Max. "Keep your hand completely flat."

Neapolitano Africa pricked his ears forward as he reached out and gently took the grass. His lips felt like velvet as they brushed across Kurt's hand. Then the horse whickered gently and nuzzled Kurt's pockets, searching for more.

Kurt laughed and pushed him away, running his fingers through the horse's flowing white mane. He loved Africa. All the stallions were beautiful, but this one was special. He was so gentle and intelligent. Max said he used to be one of the best when the Spanish Riding School gave their displays.

Suddenly they heard someone run into

the yard and a voice shouted, "The Americans! The Americans are coming."

Kurt felt another shiver of fear and he noticed Max looked anxious too. What would these strange soldiers be like? How would they behave and, most important of all, what would they do with the horses?

Max handed him a broom. "Americans or no Americans, the horses still need looking after. Let's keep busy. It'll stop us worrying."

Kurt set to work to sweep the yard and he was just finishing when two men walked in. One of them was a stranger in a strange uniform, but the other was the Colonel. Max liked him. He was the head of the Spanish Riding School and he had brought the horses from Vienna to the safety of St Martin.

The stranger smiled at Kurt and held out something wrapped in paper. Kurt wasn't sure what to do but the Colonel nodded

 encouragingly so he reached out and took the present. It was chocolate – a whole bar of chocolate – and he hadn't had chocolate for months and months.

He slipped back to the stable and gave a piece to Africa. Then he put another in his mouth and felt the delicious, sweet smoothness of it trickling down his throat.

Max walked up smiling. "That was an American officer who has heard of the Spanish Riding School," he said. "He wants us to put on a performance for his General. If the horses can show him how clever they are, maybe the General will do something to save them."

They only had two days to get everything ready. Kurt helped some of the other villagers to clean up the indoor riding arena. It was in an old barn which looked very run-down and neglected. So they cut greenery from the woods, carried it into the arena and used it to hide the shabbiness of the walls.

While Kurt worked, he caught glimpses of the horses and riders practising. The white stallions looked wonderful with their arched necks and flowing manes and tails. They trotted and cantered more gracefully than any horse Kurt had seen before, moving in perfect harmony with their riders. Surely the General would love these beautiful animals.

The day before the performance, Kurt helped Max unpack the saddles and bridles the horses would wear. He was very careful with them as some of the saddles were almost 300 years old.

Max held out a bridle trimmed with brass. "You can clean this one," he said. "It's Africa's."

Kurt worked hard and soon the bridle looked beautiful. The leather was soft and supple and the brass gleamed like gold in the sunlight. He closed his eyes and imagined Africa wearing it. Then he looked at Max and asked, "What will happen if the General doesn't like the horses?"

Max bit his lip nervously. "I don't know," he said. "But without his help, something dreadful might happen. They may be taken to pull carts or even killed for meat."

His words filled Kurt with fear. He couldn't bear the thought of losing Africa. But he knew there was nothing he could do. Everything depended on the General.

The next morning Kurt ran to the old barn to find a good place to watch the display. But an American soldier stopped him at the door. "You can't come in here," he said. "No one is allowed in except General Patton and the other guests."

Kurt's eyes widened in dismay. This might be the last chance he ever had to see Africa and the other stallions perform. He couldn't miss it. Somehow he must get inside.

He waited until the soldier was
looking the other way and then crept
round the back of the building. Luckily
there were no soldiers there. He climbed
quietly through a broken window and
slipped into the empty barn. Then he hid
behind some of the greenery and waited.

A few minutes later, the visitors arrived.
The General was tall and thin. He was
wearing a uniform with knee-length boots
and he was carrying a camera.

As soon as he was settled in his seat, the

performance began. A line of eight white stallions walked down the centre of the arena with their necks arched proudly and their ears pricked forward. Their coats gleamed from hours of grooming and their riders were dressed in the traditional brown and cream uniform of the Spanish Riding School.

To Kurt's dismay, the General leant back in his chair and put his hand in front of his mouth to hide a yawn. He seemed bored and showed little interest in the horses as they walked towards him. But then someone turned on a record  player and the horses started to trot slowly in perfect time with the music. The General sat up straighter and started to pay more attention.

The horses moved gracefully around the old barn, first at a trot and then in a slow, collected canter. At the furthest corner from the General, they turned and came diagonally across the arena, criss-crossing their legs like ballet dancers – each horse perfectly in step with his companions.

Kurt was breathless with excitement. It was the most magical sight he had ever seen. The horses were moving so lightly over the ground that they seemed to be dancing to the music. It was as if they understood how important the performance was and they were dancing for their lives.

The General was obviously enchanted by them, too. He leaned forward so as not to miss any detail of the elegant performance and watched the horses with unbroken concentration.

The horses split into two groups,

cantering in opposite directions as they made patterns of circles and figures of eight. Then they came back together again, still moving as gracefully as before and still perfectly in step.

Kurt would happily have watched them for ever, but eventually the music finished and so did the dance. The line of stallions left and two fresh horses walked in to the opening notes of a new tune.

The two stallions stopped in front of the General and the riders raised their hats in salute. Then the stallions started their part of the performance – a spectacular display of the most difficult movements they could do. Kurt watched with amazement as they balanced perfectly on their hind legs and leapt forward several steps before they put their front feet down. Then they leapt high into the air with all four feet off the

ground and, at the top of their leap, they kicked out hard with their back legs.

After the two stallions finished their display, other horses and riders demonstrated their skills until finally it was Africa's turn. He came into the arena at a high stepping trot. His muscles rippled under his gleaming, white coat and the light glinted from the polished brass on his bridle. Kurt had never seen him look so beautiful before.

The Colonel sat motionless in Africa's saddle, holding the reins in only one hand. Together the two of them gave a wonderful display of riding to music – the best of the whole performance. But when they had finished, the Colonel didn't ride out of the arena as the others had done. Instead he rode right up to the General and asked him to save the horses.

The General looked surprised. He turned round and had a whispered conversation with the men sitting next to him. Then he stood up and smiled. "These horses are magnificent," he said. "The United States Army will protect them."

Kurt wanted to shout with delight, but he stopped himself just in time. He didn't want to be discovered. Instead, he slipped out through the hole in the wall and ran round to meet Africa as he came out of the arena.

He threw his arms round the horse's neck, buried his face in the flowing white mane and said, "You're safe, Africa. You're all safe."

General Patton and the American Army kept the white horses safe until Austria was peaceful again. Eventually the horses returned to Vienna and now their descendants give performances which delight visitors to the Spanish Riding School.

Did you know...?

Horse breeds

1. The white stallions of the Spanish Riding School are all Lippizaners descended from the original Spanish horses which give the School its name. They are born with dark coats but these gradually lighten until they eventually turn white. Occasionally one of the horses stays dark and, by tradition, the School includes one dark stallion in its team.

2. The only breed of horses in the world which has never been domesticated is the Przewalski horse (pronounced *she-val-ski*). It comes from the mountains between China and Mongolia and its mane stands

up straight like a donkey's. Sadly there are none left in the wild today.

3. Near the end of the 18th century, there was a stallion called Justin Morgan who was so strong that he easily won many weight-pulling competitions. The foals he fathered inherited all his good points and so did their foals. Eventually his descendants formed the breed we call the Morgan Horse.

4. Every English Thoroughbred can trace his family back through the generations to at least one of three great stallions – the Darley Arabian, the Byerley Turk and the Godolphin Arabian. Although he is now one of the most famous horses in the history of horse breeding, the Godolphin

Arab pulled a cart round the streets of Paris before he came to England.

5. American Appaloosas are famous for their spotted coats, but they don't all look the same. Some have leopard spots which are dark on a white background. Others have snowflake markings which are white spots on a dark background. If an Appaloosa only has a patch of spots on its rump, it is called blanket spotted.

6. The largest horses in the world are Shires. Some of them are more than 180 cm high and they are all very strong and very gentle. Their feet look even larger than they really are because the lower parts of their legs are covered with long hair called feathers.

Shipwreck

Western Australia, 1 December 1876

Grace looked up from the dried fruit she was preparing and wiped the sweat from her forehead with her sleeve. It was stiflingly hot in the kitchen despite the strong wind blowing in from the sea. Christmas pudding-making wasn't suited to the heat of an Australian summer.

"Do I have to do this now, Mamma?" she said. "Can't I go riding instead?"

Mrs Bussell shook her head. Then she looked at her daughter's red face and added sympathetically, "But you can go outside for a moment, if you like."

It was cooler on the porch. The wind whistled round the house, whipped at the treetops and sent dust scurrying across the yard. There was a taste of salt in the air blown in from the foaming tops of the waves. It made Grace think of how frightening the sea would be today and she breathed a sigh of relief that she was safe on dry land.

Suddenly Sam Isaacs ran into the yard and raced towards the house. He was waving at her and yelling something. But the wind snatched the words from his mouth and blew them away.

Her mother must have seen the young man coming for she came out to meet him as he ran up the steps to the porch. "Whatever's the matter, Sam," she said when she saw his anxious face.

"It's a ship, Mrs Bussell," he gasped breathlessly. "I saw it from the hill. It's being blown in to Calgardup and it'll go aground for sure."

"A shipwreck," gasped Grace with a

shiver of excitement. She'd read about wrecks in books. Now there was going to be a real one so close that she would be able to see it.

"Oh, those poor people," said Mrs Bussell. "If anyone survives, they'll need our help. We'll take the cart up to fetch them."

Grace's eyes opened wide in horror as she thought of the desperate passengers struggling in the pounding waves. The bullock cart was so slow. It would never reach the beach in time to save them. "We must do more than that," she said. "Let me go ahead, Mamma. I can get there so much quicker if I ride."

Her mother hesitated.

"Please. You don't have to worry. I'm sixteen now and I ride as well as any boy."

"And I'll go with her," said Sam. "She won't be on her own."

Mrs Bussell nodded reluctantly. "All

right," she said. "Go and do what you can. But be careful, both of you."

There was no time to waste. As Grace ran to the stables with Sam, she pulled off her apron and threw it to the ground. There would be no more pudding-making today. A much bigger adventure lay ahead.

Sam swiftly fetched his favourite horse, Bess. Grace chose her father's chestnut gelding, Smiler – a huge, gentle animal who was faster and stronger than her own little mare. He greeted her with a welcoming whicker and nuzzled her pockets for sugar while she put on his bridle.

As soon as Grace and Sam were in the saddle, they pushed the horses into a gallop and headed for the stricken ship. Smiler and Bess seemed to sense the urgency of their task. They stretched their necks forward as they raced across the open ground. The wind whipped at their manes and their hooves pounded on the dry soil.

Grace leant forward in the saddle, urging Smiler on faster and faster. The wind stung her face and lashed at the folds of her skirt. The stirrup leathers pinched her unprotected leg but she didn't care. All that mattered was reaching the wreck before everyone drowned.

They raced to the top of the sand-hills

which bordered the shore, and pulled the horses to a halt. Grace looked across the wide sandy beach to the white waters of the breakers and saw the ship for the first time.

It was trapped on the rocks about a hundred metres from the shore and broadside on to the pounding surf. One of the masts was already snapped and the wind tore at the bedraggled remnants of its sails.

It wasn't the wind that was the real danger now. It was the sea. Powerful waves crashed over the ship again and again, sweeping the deck with tumbling water. There was no way the wreck could survive such a battering for long and, when it broke up, anyone still on board would drown.

Suddenly Sam pointed. "Look," he yelled above the roar of the wind and waves. "They're launching a lifeboat."

Grace bit her lip anxiously as she watched the rowing boat drop into the restless sea. It looked so tiny tossing up and down beside the main ship; but this was all that stood between most of the passengers and certain death. Only the strongest swimmers would manage to reach the shore without it.

Suddenly, just as the crew began to row, a huge wave caught the little boat and sent it rushing towards the beach. For a moment, it looked as if it might reach the shore safely. Then the white crest of the wave crashed down on the boat and turned it over, throwing everyone on board into the tumbling surf.

Grace could hear their screams above the booming roar of the waves. "We've got to save them," she yelled. "If we ride into the sea, we might be able to pull them out."

She urged Smiler into action and the horse leapt forward, plunging down the steep slope towards the beach. His hooves slithered and slipped on the loose sandy soil. For a moment,

Grace feared that he would fall and be trampled by Bess, who was following close behind. But, with a huge effort, he managed to keep his footing and reach the bottom safely.

As soon as they were on the beach, Grace and Sam pushed their horses into a gallop again. They raced side by side across the wide stretch of sand as they had often done before for pleasure. But this time, they were racing for real – people's lives depended on them.

Grace peered ahead through eyes half-closed against the wind-blown sand. The waves were far bigger than they had looked from the hill. Each one became steeper and steeper as it rolled towards the shore – a rising wall of water which foamed white along its crest before it crashed down and surged up the beach with a tumbling roar.

Her mouth went dry with fear. Surf like

this was dangerous and she was small and powerless. How could she hope to rescue anyone from such a sea?

Soon the horses' hooves were splashing through the shallow froth on the edge of the breakers. Smiler hesitated as he saw the white water of the waves ahead of him and Grace knew this was the moment when she had to make her decision. Should she risk her own life and Smiler's to save these strangers or should she surrender to her fear and leave them there to die?

But as soon as she thought of turning back, she realized she couldn't. She had already come this far. Maybe with Smiler's strength to help her, there was a chance of saving someone. She couldn't give up now.

She pressed her legs against the chestnut's sides and he plunged forward bravely into the tumbling white water. Then the next wave came, breaking over their heads with such force that Grace had to grab hold of the saddle to stop herself being swept from Smiler's back. For a moment, she was completely under water. Then, as the wave rushed on towards the beach, her head came clear of the surface and she took a huge gasp of air. She glanced sideways and saw Sam beside her on Bess, his clothes soaking wet and sticking to his body. But then another breaker came and they were lost from view again.

Smiler battled on valiantly towards the capsized boat. Each new wave lifted him off his feet, forcing him to swim until the wall of water passed and his hooves touched bottom again. As he moved further and further from the shore, the water grew deeper and he had to swim all the time – sometimes sheltered in the troughs of the waves and sometimes carried up high into the full force of the wind.

Grace looked around anxiously, searching for any sign of life. Suddenly, she saw a man struggling to keep afloat and turned  Smiler towards him. As they came closer, she held out her hand and yelled, "Grab hold of me."

He reached out desperately and nearly touched her fingers. But the next wave came and swept him away before she could get closer. He disappeared under the water and, for a moment, Grace feared that he had drowned. But a couple of seconds later he surfaced, spluttering and gasping for breath. Smiler swam up to him again and this time the man managed to grab a stirrup.

"Hold tight," she yelled and headed the horse back towards the shore.

As she did so, she spotted another man in the water just ahead of her. But before Smiler could swim up to him, a huge wave came, lifting the horse up and sweeping him towards the beach. "Grab hold of me," yelled Grace again as they

 surged towards the swimmer.

The man reached out to grasp her outstretched hand but missed. He tried again, desperate to save himself, and this time managed to grab a handful of Smiler's tail. The chestnut horse didn't even flinch, and he seemed to understand the importance of his task.

Soon Grace and the two men were safely on the shore. Sam and Bess were already there with a bedraggled sailor they had just pulled from the waves.

"There's still people on the ship," Sam shouted above the wind. "We've got to get them off before it breaks up."

He and Grace turned their horses towards the sea again and urged them back into the pounding surf. The animals were tiring a little now, but they still plunged back bravely into the foaming water.

They tried to head straight for the battered remains of the ship, but it was a difficult task. The powerful waves lifted the two horses, sweeping them back and forth in the restless sea and driving them off course. But they battled on as best they could, struggling to spot the wreck in the brief lulls between each fresh wall of water.

The wind whistled through the ship's rigging and the battered timbers groaned under the constant attack of the waves. Tumbling water surged across the deck and the frightened passengers clung tightly to the rails to stop themselves being swept away.

Grace was the first to reach the wreck. The sight of her and Sam gave the passengers the courage to try to save themselves. One by one they climbed over the side of the ship into the raging sea. The strongest swimmers set off for the shore by themselves but the others struggled towards the horses, clutching at manes, tails, stirrups and legs – anything they could hold to keep themselves afloat.

Smiler and Bess were magnificent. No horses in the world could have done better than they did. They allowed the grasping hands to tug and pull at them in a way they would never normally allow. They battled against the waves with all their strength and towed the desperate passengers to safety.

But that wasn't the end of their task, for there were too many people to save in one trip. As soon as the first batch were on shore, Grace, Smiler, Sam and Bess plunged back into the sea to fetch the others. Again and again they went until there were no more screams for help and everyone was safe.

As Grace rode out of the sea for the last time, she suddenly realized how tired she was. She shivered despite the warmth of the sun as the wet folds of her skirt flapped against the saddle and her bedraggled hair dripped sea water down her neck. Her whole body ached from the exertion of the rescue and her legs were red raw from the rub of the stirrup leathers in the salty water.

But when she looked at the rescued passengers on the beach, she knew it was all worthwhile. These were the people she and Sam had set out to help and, thanks to Smiler and Bess, all of them were safe.

With the help of Grace, Sam and the two horses, more than 50 people came safely ashore that day from the wreck of *The Georgette*. Grace's bravery earned her a silver medal from the Royal Humane Society – an award very rarely given to a woman. In addition, she was given an engraved gold watch by the British Government. Sam received a bronze medal for his part in the rescue.

Did you know...?

Horse sense

1. In the wild, horses have to be constantly alert. There is always the chance that a lion or some other predator is sneaking up on them in search of a tasty meal. That's why horses seem such nervous animals. Thousands of years of being hunted have taught them to run quickly from anything suspicious, without waiting to check if it is just a plastic bag.

2. A horse is well designed to spot danger coming. Its eyes are on the sides of its head so it can see nearly all the way round itself without moving. The only places it can't

see are a small area just in front of its face and a larger area behind its back legs. If you want to avoid startling a horse, walk up to it from the side so it can see you coming.

3. Horses don't sleep for eight hours a night like us. They prefer shorter periods of sleep spread over the whole 24 hours and often move about and graze at night. They can do this easily because their large eyes help them to see much better in the dark than we do.

4. Horses hear better than humans and can move their ears to find the direction of a sound. When you are riding, your horse may turn his ears back to listen to you. But be careful if he puts them flat back against

his neck. That means he is angry and about to bite or kick.

5. If you look in a horse's mouth, you will see two groups of teeth. The incisors for biting grass are at the front of his mouth, while the molars for chewing food are at the back. Between the two is a space with no teeth at all which is just about level with the corner of his lips. That's where the bit sits when you are riding. If you slip your thumb in there when you are putting on the bridle, he will open his mouth so you can put the bit in easily.

Foinavon's National

Aintree Racecourse, Liverpool, England, Saturday 8 April 1967

Foinavon nuzzled the white goat beside him. Susie bleated gently in response. She and the brown horse were old friends. They travelled everywhere together and she always shared his stable.

John Buckingham smiled as he watched them together. The horse looked so relaxed despite the hustle and bustle of the racecourse stables. That was good. John was nervous enough for both of them.

In a little while, he would be riding Foinavon in the Grand National – four-and-a-half miles of fast galloping over 30 huge jumps.

All the experts were sure they wouldn't win, but John didn't care. This was the greatest horse-race in the country – maybe the greatest in the world. He had always dreamt of riding in it and this afternoon his dream was going to come true.

He gave Foinavon a farewell pat and went to get ready for the race. By the time he had changed into his brightly coloured silk shirt, the atmosphere at Aintree was electric. The Grand National would soon be starting. Thousands of people jostled for a good view of the course while the television cameras prepared to broadcast the race to millions of viewers at home.

John stood in the middle of the paddock with the other jockeys and watched the horses being led round. His stomach was churning with excitement and his mouth was dry. Some of the horses were showing signs of nerves, too – snorting down their noses and dancing sideways to avoid imagined dangers. Foinavon walked round with his ears pricked. He took an interest in everything that was happening, but he didn't let any of it frighten him.

"Foinavon doesn't stand a chance," said one of the other jockeys.

"Everyone's sure he'll lose," said another.

"I don't care," said John. "He's a great horse and he'll do his best. I can't ask more than that."

John was glad when they were told to get on their horses. He felt calmer as soon as he was in the saddle. The waiting was over and it was time to get on with the riding.

After a brief parade in front of the crowd, they all turned and cantered steadily towards the start. Foinavon behaved beautifully and took no notice of the people standing beside the course.

John leant forward and patted him on the neck. He felt the strong muscles beneath the gleaming coat and was glad the horse was so fit and strong. The race ahead was going to test that fitness to the limit.

The horses lined up behind the

starting tapes stretched across the course, and John's excitement soared. The jockeys either side of him were so close that their knees were nearly touching his. John could hear the other animals snorting and stamping. He could feel the tension in Foinavon as they waited for the start.

Suddenly the tapes went up and they were off – 44 horses galloping down the course towards the first fence. John leaned forward over his horse's neck, feeling the strong pull on the bit and the rhythmic pounding of his hooves on the turf. Foinavon was going well and was up with the leaders.

The first fence loomed ahead like a living green wall. Like all the jumps on this course, it was solidly made of logs piled together and covered with branches of spruce. If a horse hit it, the horse would fall – not the fence.

The horses sped towards it. Foinavon gathered himself, took off and cleared it easily.

He landed perfectly and thundered on towards the next. But the leading horses were going so fast that he couldn't keep up with them. He gradually dropped further and further behind.

John wasn't worried. He was sure the horses at the front could not keep up such a punishing speed for the whole race. Eventually they would have to slow down and he would have a chance to catch up.

They raced on, clearing jump after jump and soon they were sweeping towards Becher's Brook – the most famous jump. He knew they had to jump Becher's again on the second time round, but for now he put that out of his mind and concentrated on the jumps immediately ahead. The thunder of hooves filled his ears and he thrilled to the feeling of speed and power as they raced around the course.

Foinavon continued to jump perfectly.

Soon Valentine's Brook, the Chair and the water jump were behind them and they swept around a sharp left-hand bend to begin their second circuit. Ahead of them, the leaders were still setting a fast pace. Right out at the front were two riderless horses whose jockeys had fallen off. Their herd instincts kept them galloping with the

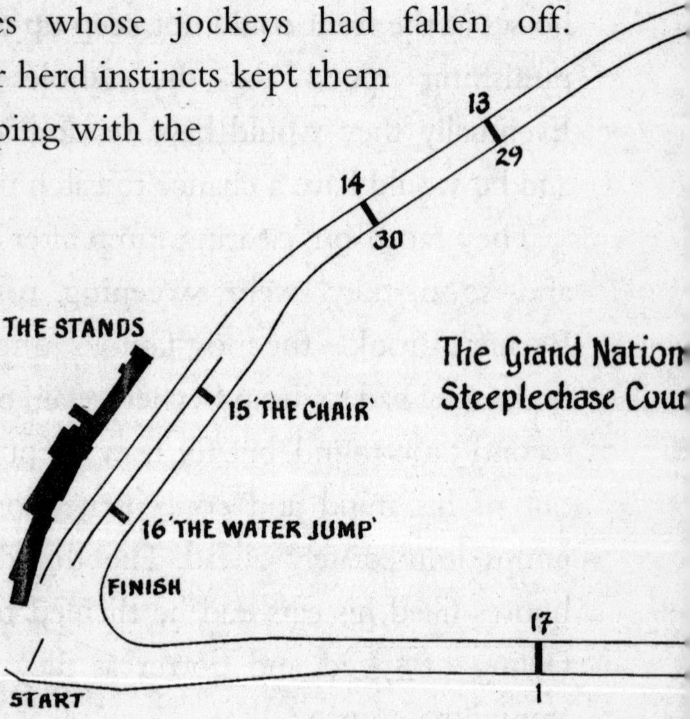

13
29
14
30

THE STANDS

15 'THE CHAIR'

The Grand Nation
Steeplechase Cour

16 'THE WATER JUMP'

FINISH

17

START

1

100

others, and they could outrun them all because they had no weight on their backs.

Foinavon was in 20th place as they came into Becher's Brook for the second time. John was delighted to see that only a few metres ahead of them was Josh Gifford of Honey End, the favourite to win the race. He knew Josh was

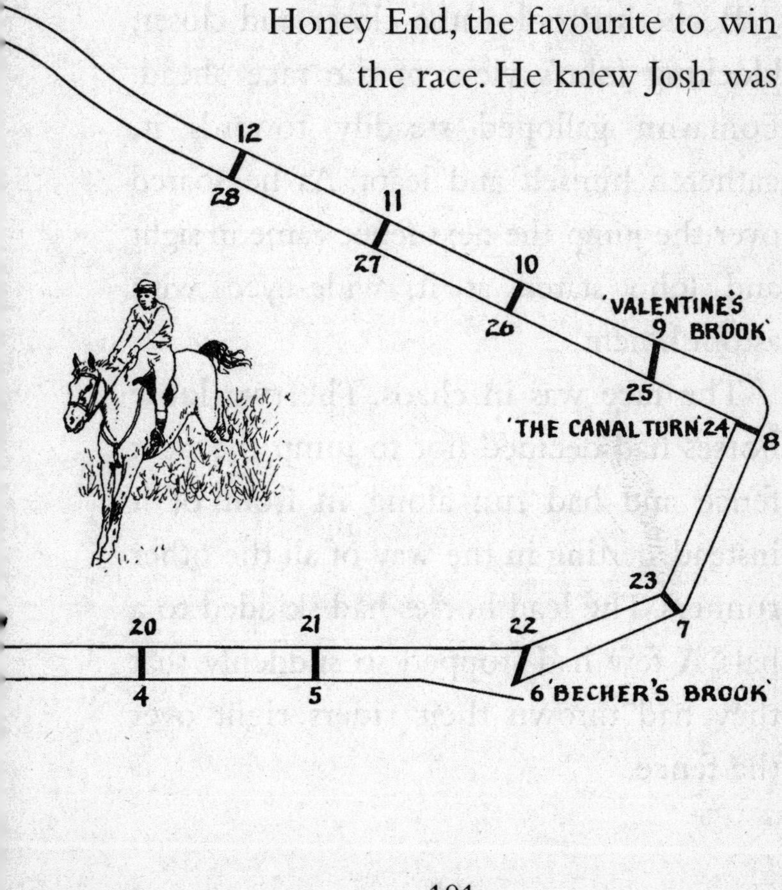

12
28
11
27
10
26
VALENTINE'S
9 BROOK
25
'THE CANAL TURN 24
8
23
20 21 22 7
4 5 6 'BECHER'S BROOK'

one of the best judges of pace in the racing world. If he thought there was still time for Honey End to catch up, there was still a chance that Foinavon would do better than everyone expected. Maybe they could finish 11th or 12th instead of last.

Becher's Brook came closer and closer, blocking John's view of the race ahead. Foinavon galloped steadily towards it, gathered himself and leapt. As he soared over the jump, the next fence came in sight and John stared at it, wide-eyed with astonishment.

The race was in chaos. The two loose horses had decided not to jump the next fence and had run along in front of it instead, getting in the way of all the other runners. The lead horses had skidded to a halt. A few had stopped so suddenly that they had thrown their riders right over the fence.

Some of the animals had crashed into the jump – pieces of spruce were scattered about and a couple of fallen horses lay among the branches, uninjured and struggling to get back on their feet.

The horses between John and the leaders were thrown into confusion. Some could not stop in time and crashed into the ones ahead. Others saw the chaos and panicked, refusing to go anywhere near it despite the efforts of their jockeys. Honey End stopped straight in front of Foinavon and whirled round, determined to go in the opposite direction.

But Foinavon stayed calm. He slowed down and swung sideways to avoid Honey End. Then he cantered on towards the jump, winding his way through the mass of whirling horses, loose animals and fallen jockeys.

John glanced around, searching for a safe route out of the chaos. Then he spotted a place at the far end of the fence where there were no other horses and turned Foinavon towards it. There was a chance they could get over but he knew it was a slim one. The fence was designed to be jumped at a gallop but there wasn't enough clear space in front to allow them to go that fast.

Foinavon cantered slowly up to it. He

hesitated for a moment. Then he took off almost from a standstill, as if he was showjumping rather than racing.

It worked. His feet cleared the top spruce branches and he landed safely on the other side.

"Go on, you'll win," yelled one of the jockeys who had fallen right over the jump.

John urged Foinavon back into a gallop, hardly daring to believe that the jockey's words might be true. They raced on over the next fence and, as they rounded the Canal Turn, he realized that they were in the lead. The only other horses still in the race were a long way behind and there were only six fences left to jump. If they could keep going like this, they would win.

The same herd instinct that kept the riderless animals in the race would have made many horses reluctant to gallop on so far ahead of everyone else. But, once again, Foinavon was brilliant. He raced on willingly, clearing jump after jump.

Soon the last fence was behind them and they were galloping up the final straight. Foinavon was hot and tired. He was soaked with sweat and breathing hard, but he still galloped as fast as he could.

The cheers of the crowd echoed in John's ears, growing louder and louder as they pounded up the last few metres of the course. As they swept past the winning-post, the cheering became a deafening roar. Foinavon had amazed everyone. He had won the National and galloped his way into racing history.

Foinavon's victory was headline news. There had never been a Grand National like it before. Luckily, none of the horses or riders were badly hurt in the chaos and, ever since that race, the 23rd jump has been known as Foinavon's Fence.

Did you know...?

Horse-racing

1. Horse-racing is one of the oldest sports in the world. The Ancient Greeks raced horse-drawn chariots in the Olympic Games more than 2,000 years ago.

2. The only horse to win the Grand National three times was called Red Rum. His victories made him so famous that he became a celebrity, appearing on television and opening shops. When he died at the age of 30, he was buried beside the finishing-line for the Grand National, so the shadow of the winning-post falls across his grave.

3. The more weight a horse carries, the slower it can run, so racehorses need to carry as little weight as they possibly can. That's why jockeys are always short, try hard to stay slim and use special saddles which are very small and light. To help keep the weight down even more, on race days racehorses wear lightweight shoes called racing plates.

4. In the 18th century, people used to race horses across open country. They would set the course by racing from one church steeple to another, jumping all the fences and ditches which were in the way. That is why races over jumps are still called steeplechases.

5. Thoroughbreds are used for racing all over the world as they can gallop at more than 30 miles an hour. But for short races only a quarter of a mile long, American Quarter Horses are faster. They have been specially bred for this type of racing which needs animals who can start quickly and sprint fast.

6. Not all racehorses gallop. Trotting-races are popular in many countries, including America, Russia and Australia. But the horses in trotting-races aren't ridden. Instead they pull a special racing cart called a sulky.

Annie's Story

Nevada, USA, July 1997

The newborn foal lay in the grass and looked at the world for the first time. The early morning sun sent long shadows across the grass and glinted from the tumbling waters of the stream. The mountain tops looked black and purple against the dawn sky. Only the highest still had snow on their peaks at this time of year.

The foal pushed her tiny hooves against

the ground and tried to stand. But half-way up, she lost her balance and fell on her side. She tried again. This time she got her hind legs up but fell forward on to her knees. She knelt there for a moment. Then she pushed herself up with her front feet and Annie stood for the very first time.

She was very wobbly to begin with. But she soon learnt how to control her long legs and took her first steps. She nuzzled her way along her mother's side to find the teats. Then she started to suck and felt her mouth fill with warm milk.

Annie was exactly the same colour as her mother. Her coat was reddish brown, her mane and tail were black and she had four white legs and a white streak down the middle of her face. Her mane stood straight up like a brush and she whisked her short, stubby tail from side to side to keep away the flies.

Her mother led her back to join the rest of the herd. The wild horses were grazing in a small valley. One stood apart from the others on a higher piece of ground. He was the stallion – Annie's father.

He had chosen that spot to keep watch for danger.

Every few minutes, he stopped grazing and lifted his head. He looked around carefully and sniffed the air for signs of danger.

For the next month, Annie explored the world from the safety of her mother's side. She played with the other foals. She got to know her brother, who had been born the year before. And, most important of all, she learnt to gallop away with the others when the stallion whistled a warning.

Annie heard that warning early one morning in the middle of August. The herd reacted instantly and started to run. Annie was at the back, galloping as hard as she could to keep up with her mother.

They raced away from the danger the stallion had spotted. But their mad gallop took them across the road to Virginia City and there was a car coming. There was a squeal of brakes as it swerved violently to miss them. But they were too close. The car hit Annie's mother and killed her instantly.

The driver got out of the car and walked towards Annie with tears in his eyes. He held out his hand in an attempt to reassure her. "Poor little thing," he said. "I'm sorry. I couldn't help it."

Annie snorted suspiciously at the man. She sniffed the air and pulled her nose back in distaste from the smell of human. For a moment, she was torn between two instincts – one which told her to stay close to her mother and the other which told her to stay with the herd. Then her fear finally overcame her and she galloped away to join the other horses.

Annie felt lost and lonely without her mother. There was no one to go to when she was tired. No one to watch over her while she slept and no one to give her warm milk to drink.

Her need for milk grew stronger and stronger. She knew the other mothers in the herd had milk for their foals. Perhaps she could have some of theirs.

She wandered up to a dark brown mare and tried to suckle. But the mare walked off quickly and raised a hind foot in a half-kick to chase Annie away.

Annie tried again. This time she approached a black mare with large white splodges on her back and neck. The mare turned her rear end towards the foal and put her ears flat back against her neck. She made it obvious that Annie wasn't welcome.

But Annie's need for milk was so great that she couldn't give up. She turned her attention to a chestnut mare whose foal was completely black except for a white star in the middle of his forehead. Annie nervously thrust her nose under the mare's belly, and found the teat between her legs and began to suck. The mare turned and sniffed her gently. She seemed to understand how much the foal needed her help.

Annie felt safe again. For the next few weeks, she ran beside the chestnut mare and the black foal. She grew bigger and stronger and became much better at finding grass and leaves to eat.

But the black foal was growing too. Soon summer turned to autumn and there was less goodness in the grass. The chestnut mare found it harder and harder to make enough milk for both the hungry foals. She had done the best she could but now she could only really cope with one. So one morning, when Annie came to suckle, the mare chased her away.

Annie tried again and again. She couldn't understand what was happening. She tried the other mares but none of them would let her feed either. She stood on the edge of the herd feeling rejected and alone.

But she wasn't the only one rejected that day. The stallion had decided that her brother, Ginger, was old enough to be a threat. The mares were his and he wasn't going to allow a young colt to steal them.

The stallion trotted aggressively towards Ginger with his head up and his tail held high. As he came closer, he broke into a canter. Then he stretched out his neck and rushed at the colt with his teeth bared. At the last moment, he stopped and reared, beating at the air with his hooves.

Ginger drew back in horror. Then he turned swiftly and galloped away. Annie hesitated for a moment. She took one last look at the herd which had been her home all her life. Then she galloped after her brother.

Once the others were out of sight, the two young horses slowed to a trot. They stopped and grazed in the shade of some cottonwood trees. Then they wandered down the hill to a stream.

An unknown stallion arrived as they were drinking. Ginger looked up in alarm but this new horse wasn't a threat. He was alone too and desperate for company. The three of them sniffed noses in greeting.

They stayed together through the autumn. Annie had to manage without milk now, but Ginger and the stallion did their best to care for her. They taught her to nibble the leaves of the white sage. They showed her where to drink and they watched over her while she slept.

The nights grew colder and the three of them stood close together for warmth. Annie was amazed when the first frost came and the crisp grass crunched beneath her hooves. She sniffed suspiciously at the white-edged leaves and pushed her nose through the white outline of a spider's web.

The stallion led them down the hillside towards some buildings. Annie was reluctant to go. She smelt humans there and the smell brought back the fear of that August morning. But she trusted the stallion and followed him warily.

There was hay there put out by

the people who lived in the two houses. It tasted sweet and good, so Annie and her friends stayed and ate their fill before they went back to the hills. They came back often, building up their strength. It would soon be time to travel down into the far valley away from the cold mountain winter.

But one morning before they were due to leave, Annie bucked playfully on the frosty grass and slipped. She fell and landed heavily on her left hind leg. When she stood up again, she found that leg hurt every time she put her weight on it. There was no way she could make the journey to the valley.

Ginger and the stallion stayed with her but they could do nothing to help. Her leg got worse and worse as the first snow fell on the mountains. She could only walk slowly, one painful step at a time. She couldn't get to the stream to drink or paw away the snow to find leaves and grass to eat.

As she grew weaker and weaker, she remembered the hay and water behind the houses. If she could get there, she might be all right. Very slowly but with great determination, she started hobbling down the hillside.

It took a long time. Often the pain got so bad that she had to stop and rest. But as soon as she felt better, she started moving again down the slope towards her only hope of safety.

She could see the houses ahead of her. There were lights shining in the windows and the sound of Christmas carols drifted towards her on the cold air. She could smell the humans but it didn't frighten her any more. The hay smelt of humans too and the hay was good.

Summoning the last of her strength, she staggered forward a few more steps and collapsed.

"Come quick," someone shouted. "There's a foal outside."

Annie heard footsteps running towards her and kind voices saying words she didn't understand. Strong arms carried her to a soft, straw bed and gentle hands pushed a rubber teat into her mouth. It tasted strange and she resisted it at first. Then she sucked at it weakly and, to her delight, warm milk filled her mouth.

She sucked and sucked until her stomach was full, feeling the food and warmth bring fresh strength to her exhausted body. Then she lay back on the straw and relaxed. It was a human being who had taken her mother from her so long ago. Now these other humans had reached out to her in kindness and saved her life.

Annie was so weak when she first arrived that the people who found her feared she might not recover. But thanks to their excellent care, she grew fit and strong and the injury and infection in her leg healed completely. She still lives on the same ranch and is now the mascot of The Virginia Range Wildlife Protection Association.

Did you know…?

Foals

1. Foals grow inside their mothers for about 11 months before birth and most of them are born at night or very early in the morning. The mare likes to go away from other horses to give birth and often chooses a marshy patch of ground.

2. Foals stand up for the first time within an hour or two of being born and they can canter beside their mothers when they are only a few hours old. This rapid development is important in the wild as it helps them to keep up with the rest of the herd.

3. Like all small animals, foals need plenty of rest. They lie down flat on their sides to sleep while their mothers stand close by, protecting them from danger. It is often hard to see a sleeping foal from a distance as it is small enough to be hidden by long grass.

4. If you watch a foal carefully when it approaches another horse, you may notice that it keeps opening and shutting its mouth. This is called mouthing and is a special signal which means "Be nice to me – I'm only a baby".

5. Thoroughbreds run races when they are only two or three years old but most horses are not ridden until they are four. By then, they have finished growing and

can carry the weight of someone on their backs without hurting themselves.

6. A young horse starts its training almost as soon as it is born. It learns to be handled by people, to have its feet picked up and to be lead in a head collar. A head collar small enough for a foal is called a foal slip.